The Better Sweater
Knitting with Gwen Byrne

Book Two:
More Unique Patterns
for All Knitters

Arbor House   New York

Manufactured in the United States of America
10 9 8 7 6 5 4 3 2 1

Library of Congress Cataloging-in-Publication Data

Byrne, Gwen.
  The better sweater.
  1. Sweaters. 2. Knitting—Patterns. I. Title.
TT825.B96 1986   746.9'2   86-17348
ISBN 0-87795-846-7 (pbk. : v. 2)
              Design by Laura Hough

Contents

The Better Sweater

BASICS AND TECHNIQUES

As your friends find out that you are learning to knit, you will discover from them that each step in knitting may have a variety of techniques. I teach what I believe to be the simplest method.

To start, you need one ball of medium-weight yarn (sport or worsted weight without knots or hairy slubs, please) and a pair of 10-inch #9 single-point knitting needles.

Casting On

1. Wrap the yarn twice around two fingers and pull the lower thread up through the center to form a slip knot. Place this loop onto a knitting needle, tightening it to slide easily on the needle. Hold this needle in your left hand.
2. Insert the right-hand needle through the loop from the front to the back.
3. Wrap the yarn from under, around the right needle. Holding the yarn tightly, bring the yarn through the slip knot until this loop is about 1½ inches long.
4. Slip this loop onto the left needle to form the second stitch.
5. Insert the right-hand needle in between the first and second stitches, tightening the first stitch, and repeat Steps 3 and 4. All the stitches should be the same size on the needle.

Continue like this until you have cast on 20 stitches for your first sample.

Place the needle containing the stitches in your left hand.

The Knit Stitch (k st)

1. With the yarn hanging in the back, insert the right-hand needle into the first stitch from front to back. Wrap the yarn from under, around the right-hand needle.
2. Holding the yarn tightly, bring the yarn through the stitch, forming a new stitch on the right-hand needle, and slide the first stitch off the left-hand needle.
3. Repeat Steps 1 and 2 until all the stitches are on the right-hand needle.
4. Place the needle with the stitches in your left hand and continue with Steps 1 and 2.

When this stitch is used in every row, it is called garter stitch and is distinguishable by the ridges it forms on both sides of your sample.

The Purl Stitch (p st)

1. With the yarn hanging in the front, insert the right-hand needle into the first stitch from the back toward the front. Wrap the yarn over and around the right-hand needle.
2. Holding the yarn tightly, bring the needle through the stitch toward the back, forming a

new stitch on the right-hand needle, and slide the first stitch off the left-hand needle.
3. Repeat Steps 1 and 2 until all the stitches are on the right-hand needle.
4. Place the needle with the stitches in your left hand and continue with Steps 1 and 2.

The purl stitch is used in combination with the knit stitch; it is rarely used on its own. The stitch formed when working one row of knit and one row of purl alternately is called stockinette stitch (st st).

Work about 3 inches of stockinette stitch on your sampler and try to recognize which side is the knit side and which the purl.

Knit side: rows of V's.

Purl side: rows of loops.

By this time you probably realize that part of the art of knitting is holding the yarn with even tension so that all the stitches are the same size.

My method puts the little finger of the right hand to work, and sometimes it objects painfully. Practice, and an even group of stitches will soon replace the pain with pride.

Holding the Yarn

1. Four inches from your stitches, scoop the yarn with your little finger from back to front.

2. Twist the hand so that the thread runs in the palm of your hand.
3. Bring the index finger under the thread, bend the other fingers, and you are ready. The index finger, with the yarn across the first joint, guides the yarn, and the little finger guides the tension of the knitting.

Use the little finger:

1. Bent, when you have enough yarn in your hand; and
2. Slightly raised, when you need to feed more yarn to the index finger.

All this will feel very clumsy at first, but the clumsiness will disappear after a while.

Ribbing

Combining knit and purl stitches on the same row to form ribs is called ribbing. Generally worked with a smaller needle, ribbing forms a natural border because of its elasticity. The sweater will hold its shape better at the hip, waist, wrist, and neck areas because of the ribbing.

Here are some examples:

1 × 1 Rib: *knit 1 stitch, purl 1 stitch*
* k1, p1, * —repeat the stitches between the asterisks.

2 × 2 Rib: *knit 2 stitches, purl 2 stitches*
* k2, p2 * —repeat the stitches
between the asterisks.

This pattern will work correctly only if the yarn is at the correct place (either in front of the work or behind it) when needed.

An example of the 2 × 2 rib:

k2, bring the yarn in between the two needles toward the front, and p2. Take the yarn in between the two needles toward the back, and k2. Repeat until all the stitches have been worked.

To shape the sweater, you will need to make sections larger or smaller; this means increasing or decreasing the number of stitches.

The Increase (inc)

On a knit row:

1. Insert the right-hand needle from front to back into the loop of the stitch below the next stitch to be knitted.
2. Place this extra loop on the left-hand needle and knit the 2 stitches separately (1 inc).

On a purl row:

1. Insert the right-hand needle from front to back into the loop of the stitch below the next stitch to be purled.
2. Place this extra loop on the left-hand needle,

twisting the stitch toward the front, and purl the 2 stitches separately (1 inc).

This method of increasing is the easiest and the least obvious. Various other methods leave large and unsightly holes.

To make a section of a sweater smaller means reducing the number of stitches. This is called decreasing, and here you need to know more than one technique.

The Decrease (dec)— work 2 stitches (sts) together (tog)

On a knit row:

Insert the needle through 2 sts as to knit (knitwise). Knit them tog to form 1 st. This stitch slants to the right.

On a purl row:

Insert the needle through 2 sts as to purl (purlwise). Purl them tog to form 1 st.

The Decrease—slip (sl) a stitch

On a knit row:

1. Insert the needle into the st as to knit. Slip the st from the left-hand needle to the right (sl 1).
2. Knit the next stitch.
3. Insert the tip of the left-hand needle into the slip stitch (sl st) from left to right toward the front, holding the yarn tightly so that the knit stitch (k st) does not slide off the needle. Pass the sl st over the k st, and drop it off the needle. This stitch slants to the left.

On a purl row:

1. Insert the needle into the st as if to purl. Slip the st from the left-hand needle to the right (sl 1).
2. Purl the next st.
3. Insert the tip of the left-hand needle into the slip stitch (sl st) from left to right, toward the front, holding the yarn tightly so that the purl stitch (p st) does not slide off the needle. Pass the sl st over the p st, and drop it off the needle.

Adding New Yarn

At some point you will need to add new yarn when one skein is finished.

Always add yarn at the beginning (beg) of a row. This method can be used when attaching yarn of the same color or of another color for stripes.

1. Drop the old yarn.
2. Leaving about 8 inches of the new skein hanging, put the needle into the first stitch. Make a loop, place this onto the right-hand needle, and knit the first stitch. Finish the row.
3. Tie the new and the old threads together, tightening the few loose sts at the beg of the row. These dangling threads will be used in the finishing of the seams of your sweater. Never tie double knots, please!

To remove all the stitches from the needles with a finished edge (which prevents the sts from unraveling), you bind off.

Binding Off

Always try to bind off on the knit side, as follows:

1. Knit 2 sts.
2. Insert the left-hand needle into the front of the first st knitted, from left to right. Pass the stitch over the second stitch and drop it off the needle. This is 1 st bound off.
3. Knit 1 more stitch and repeat Step 2. Hold the thread tightly when passing one stitch over the other, but try to keep the stitches as loose as possible.

When 1 last stitch remains, cut the thread, leaving about 10 inches, and pull the thread through the stitch. This thread is used to sew the seams.

NOTE: When binding off, you always need 2 sts on the right-hand needle.

Binding Off in Pattern

On a k2, p2 rib, bind off as follows:

> k2, bind off 1 st, bring the yarn to the front, p1, take the yarn to the back, bind off 1 st. Repeat, knitting the knit stitches and purling the purl stitches.

Asterisks

These are indicators advising that the instructions within the asterisks are to be repeated. For example:

> *k2, p1, k2* repeat 1 ×. This means, k2, p1, k2, k2, p1, k2.

If no specific number of repeats is indicated, just repeat the instructions to the end of the row.

Yarn Over (y o)

Yarn over is used to make buttonholes or lacy eyelet stitches.

When the following stitch is a knit stitch:

> From the back, wrap the yarn over and under the needle toward the back, leaving 1 slanted st across the needle.

When the following stitch is a purl stitch:

> From the front, wrap the yarn over and under the needle toward the front.

Buttonholes

Here are two methods. Use the first method for small buttons.

FIRST METHOD
Work a few sts from the edge, yarn over (y o), k2 tog, work to the end of the row. On the following row, remember to knit or purl the yarn over as your pattern indicates.

SECOND METHOD
Work to the correct position in the pattern (usually 2 to 4 sts from the edge) sl 1, k1, pass the sl st over (psso). Turn your needles so that the work is facing in the opposite direction and cast on 2 sts. Turn the needles back to the original position and k2 tog, pulling the thread quite tightly

so that no holes are formed. Continue in pattern to the end of the row.

Work the next row in pattern as established before the buttonhole.

Stitch Gauge

Knitting a sample swatch to make a stitch gauge is probably the most important step when knitting a sweater. The stitch gauge is the measurement you require to tell you how many stitches equal 1 inch, and how many rows equal 1 inch. This information determines the number of stitches you will need to make your sweater the correct size.

All instructions in this book and in other books or magazines base the sizing of a sweater (or other garment) on the combination of the weight (thickness) of the yarn used, the size of the needles, and the determined stitch gauge. The smaller the needles and the thinner the yarn, the more sts and rows it will take to make 1 inch. When the needles are bigger and the yarn is thicker, you will require fewer stitches and rows per inch.

The stitch gauge is usually given for 4 inches. A swatch of this size is more accurate than a smaller one.

Never measure the gauge by the border or rib stitch; this would not be an accurate measurement. Always use the larger needles and the stitch suggested for the body of the sweater to make a swatch.

Making a Swatch

Using the needles, yarn, and stitch pattern specified in the instructions, cast on the number of sts for 4 inches plus 4 extra sts. Work a swatch about 4 inches long. Bind off all the sts. Smooth out the sample on a table. *DO NOT STRETCH THE SWATCH.*

Using a knit measure gauge (more accurate than a tape measure), measure the required number of stitches and the required number of rows. If your swatch is smaller than 4 inches wide, change to larger needles and knit a new swatch. Check the gauge again. If the swatch is larger than 4 inches wide, change to smaller needles and repeat the procedure. Measure the swatch again. Repeat this until the gauge is correct.

This procedure should never be omitted. Always knit a swatch. It is far more sensible to take the time to knit a swatch than to rip a too small or too large sweater later.

Picking Up Stitches

Stitches are picked up to create a border around the armholes or neck, or the fronts of a cardigan.

A circular needle 16 inches long is used for crew necks and one 24 inches long is used for V necks.

1. Starting at the left shoulder, with the right side of the sweater facing you, insert the needle 1 st from the edge, straight through toward the back. Wrap the yarn around the needle and bring this st through toward the front. Repeat this step until all the sts have been picked up on the side edge.
2. At the center front of the neck and along the back, the bound-off sts are treated in the same way. The needle is inserted under both bound-off yarns.

This is a tricky procedure. One hint is to keep the needle tip short so that the distance between the sts on the needle and the st to be picked up is minimal.

3. When all the sts are on the needle, place a ring marker on the needle to show the beginning of the round. Start working in the pattern as instructed. These sts are always worked in rounds. Do not turn the needles back and forth after the round is completed.
4. For armhole borders, use straight single-pointed needles. Use circular needles only if the side seams of the sweater have been sewn together.

Markers

Markers are used to indicate special places on a garment, such as armholes. There are two kinds of markers.

1. A piece of thread or a coil marker, which are used for armhole indicators. These markers will be removed when the sweater is being sewn together.
2. For division on a knitting needle, as an indicator of a certain number of stitches or a stitch pattern, use a regular flat ring marker. This does not get knitted into the sweater but moves from needle to needle as you work. It is a cue to you that the pattern stitch changes.

Measuring

Always measure any piece of the sweater straight up or sideways, never at an angle. To measure the width while you are working, work the border and 3 inches of the sweater. Spread the work onto two needles and then measure the width. Now you can tell what the piece measures before it reaches the required length and you realize that it is too small or too large.

Lengths, not only widths, are also important. If you are long-waisted or short-waisted, changes have to be made. This length adjustment is generally made before the armhole shaping or before the marker is placed in position.

To make measuring an armhole length easier, you can follow the colored thread hint. When you work the first decrease on the sleeve, work along with your yarn a 10-inch thread of another color, knitting about 10 sts in the middle of the row. This forms an obvious line, which makes measuring the armhole length or the sleeve cap very easy. This thread is removed when the sleeve has been set into the sweater.

Yarn Substitution

Each sweater in this book has been made in the specified yarn. If this yarn is not available to you, ask your yarn store or supplier to recommend a substitute. In selecting a substitute, however, I have an added simple recommendation: buy one skein of a yarn you like, and go home and knit swatches with different needle sizes. This will serve two purposes: to make sure you can get the correct gauge and to feel the draping quality of the yarn. Following this procedure will eliminate all those ill-fitting garments that lie in the bottom of your drawers. If the gauge is correct but the swatch seems too sheer or too dense, choose another yarn. Refer to Check-It-Up (page 000) to see what happens when two totally different yarns are used to make the same sweater. One version, made with a soft angora, drapes readily; the other, made of a heavier, dense cotton, does not drape at all. Both are beautiful, but the same pattern has yielded two quite different sweaters.

A Schematic

A schematic is a linear sketch of the garment and its shape. Along each edge is an arrow with an inch measurement. This tells you the width or length of any given section of the body or sleeve of the garment. Understanding the schematic serves two very important purposes:

1. It illustrates the shape of the piece you are knitting; it is especially useful if complicated shaping is required.
2. It helps you decide on the length or width or general size of any given part of the sweater in case you want to make adjustments.

PLEASE always read the schematic. It is a vital part of the sweater you are knitting. Understanding the schematic will erase the "my sweater does not fit" syndrome. Never knit happily along without checking the measurements.

Choosing a Size

Always refer to the FINISHED MEASUREMENTS before deciding on the size to knit. Large sweaters are fashionable now, and the size of the sweater does not correspond to your actual size. This should be considered when using all patterns from magazines and books.

Shaping

The language used for shaping armholes and necks can be almost as confusing as trying to read a schematic for the first time. I hope these descriptions will clarify these points.

Sewing a Sweater Together

When putting a sweater together, always work at a table—a flat surface is much better than a bed or a rug.

The first step is to pin the pieces together with sturdy straight pins. Begin with the shoulders: starting at the arm edge, with the right sides of the pieces facing each other, place one or two pins. Next, pin the neck edge. Finally, ease and pin the center pieces of fabric. Continue in this fashion with all the pieces: always pinning the outer edges first, and then easing and pinning the midsections.

To sew, use a blunt-tip embroidery needle or yarn needle and threads hanging from the sweater, if possible. Using a running stitch, insert the needle one stitch from the edge, from the front through both pieces of work, to the back. Pull the needle and thread through. Then insert the needle from the back to the front into the very next stitch, *never skip any stitches*, pull the needle and thread through to the front. Repeat until the seam is complete. Tension of the stitch should allow the same elasticity as exists in the garment. When you run out of thread, weave the needle and thread backward through the top of the seam and cut the end that remains. When attaching a new thread, repeat the last two inches sewn to create an overlap and prevent gaps in the seam.

When you want absolutely flat seams, to attach a pocket for example, use a back or over stitch.

Finishing a Drop-Shoulder Sweater

1. With the right sides of back and front facing, pin and sew the shoulder seams.
2. Open and lay out flat the back and front with the right side facing up. The yarn or coil markers will still be attached to the sweater.
3. Fold the sleeve in half to find the center of the bound-off edge (the wider side of the length of the sleeve). With the right side facing down, pin the center of the bound-off edge of the sleeve to the shoulder seam of the sweater. The sleeve is now lying across the sweater, covering the neck opening. The bound-off edge of the sleeve will be parallel to the side edge of the sweater, lining up with the markers. Pin the sleeve into the area between the marker on the front and the marker on the back. Pin the body and the sleeve together,

being careful not to stretch one side more than the other. Sew the seam.
4. Fold the sweater so that the right side is on the inside. Starting at the underarm, pin the sleeve seams and then the side seams. Sew the seams.

Finishing a Sweater with a Shaped Armhole/Cap Sleeve

1. With the right sides facing, sew the shoulder seams, the sleeve seams, and the sweater side seams.
2. With the wrong side of the sweater facing you, turn the sleeve right side out. Slide the sleeve through the armhole into the inside of the sweater.
3. Center the sleeve seam and the sweater side seam, pinning them together. Center the shoulder seam and the center of the sleeve cap and pin them together. Now ease the sleeve cap into the armhole, pinning all the way around before you sew. Sew.

Cables

Cables always look professional and appear complicated to make. The actual cable twist is, however, one of the simplest knitting techniques.

You need a cable needle (c n), which is a short straight or curved needle with points on both sides.

RULES FOR A CABLE TWIST

1. Cables always twist on the knit side of the specified cable stitches.
2. Cables always consist of an even number of stitches.

These two rules can be changed, but very seldom are.

HOW TO CABLE (8 STS)

Place 4 sts onto the c n and hold the c n at the back of the work (this cable will twist to the right), k the next 4 sts, pulling tightly to close the space, then k the sts from the c n.

DO NOT TWIST THE CABLE NEEDLE. The stitches slide on from one side and are worked off from the other side.

The cable twist occurs on a specified row and is repeated on that row only, not on every row. For example: every 6th row or every 8th row, or whichever row the instructions name.

For the rows in between the cable twist row, follow the stitches in the pattern that has

11

been established; that is, knit the knits and purl the purls.

To make the cable twist to the left, hold the cable needle at the front of the work.

The Neck Edge

This term applies to the edge at either side of the sts bound off for the neck in the center of a crew neck *or* on the center edges when working a V neck shaping. When shaping a crew or V neck, the two sides of the front are worked at the same time, on the same needle, but you attach another skein of yarn so that each shoulder has its own thread. Therefore the two pieces are worked separately but *at the same time.*

On the left shoulder, the neck edge is at the beginning of the row.

On the right shoulder, the neck edge is at the end of the row, *but* both neck edges are in the center section of the sweater, not at the outer edges. If you are making a cardigan, one side (you decide which) will be the neck edge and the other side will be the armhole edge. Remember that cardigans have two front pieces, which should be the opposite of each other.

The Armhole Edge

This term applies to the outer edge of every back and front if the sweater is a pullover; if it is a cardigan, the armhole edge is at the outer edge of each front piece.

A Sweater in One Piece

This method requires concentrated shaping techniques, creating sweaters knitted in different directions. For example:

1. Start at the left wrist, knit one sleeve first, shaping as you knit along; cast on for the body (both back and front) and then bind off both back and front stitches after the piece measures the desired length; finish the sweater with the correct reversed shaping for the right sleeve, ending at the right wrist.
2. Start at the front (or back) waist or hip, work straight until casting on for the two sleeves, over the shoulders, until binding off for the sleeves; complete the length on the back (or front) and end at the waist or hip.

With each of these techniques, the separation for the neck is the only time you work one half of the stitches at a time. You rejoin the garment when both sides have been worked separately but are of equal lengths.

Always use long, flexible needles when working these large pieces.

Abbreviations

beg	beginning
c n	cable needle
dec	decrease
inc	increase
k	knit
p	purl
rev	reverse
r s	right side
sl	slip
sl 1, k1, psso	slip 1 stitch, knit 1 stitch, pass the slip stitch over
ssk	slip 1st and 2nd stitches knitwise, knit together with left-hand needle passed through the fronts of the stitches
st	stitch
st st	stockinette stitch
tog	together
wyib	with the yarn in the back
wyif	with the yarn in the front
w s	wrong side
yb	yarn back
yf	yarn forward
yo	yarn over
1×	one time

Patterns

BEGINNER

July Fourth

SIZES: Small, medium; medium size is in parentheses

FINISHED MEASUREMENTS: Bust 37 (40) inches; total length 19 (21) inches

MATERIALS:
Lane Borgosesia Tuttimesi 4 (50 g/1.75 ounce) skeins, pink
Fantacia Sardinia 5 (50 g/1.75 ounce) skeins, white/pink/yellow
These two yarns are used together throughout the sweater.
Needles: #6, #9 single-point

GAUGE: 14 sts and 18 rows = 4 inches
(3.5 sts = 1 inch; 4.5 rows = 1 inch)
Please check your gauge.

STITCH PATTERNS:
Stockinette stitch

BACK

With smaller needles (#6) and 1 strand of each yarn, cast on 60 sts. Work k1, p1 rib for 3 inches. Change to larger needles (#9) and st st and inc 6 (10) sts evenly across the first knit row (66 [70] sts). Work until piece measures 11 (12) inches. Shape the armhole as follows: Bind off 4 sts at the beg of the next 2 rows. Dec 1 st at each edge 4× (48 [54] sts). Place yarn markers at each edge when piece measures 14½ inches. Work until armhole measures 7 (8) inches. Now work k1, p1 rib for 1 inch. Bind off all sts loosely in pattern.

FRONT

Repeat the back.
Sew shoulders tog, leaving a 9-inch neck opening.

CAP SLEEVE

With #9 needles and with the right side facing you, pick up 32 sts in between the markers. In st st work 1 row, picking up 2 more sts at the end of the row. Repeat this last row until 70 sts have been picked up around the entire armhole. Change to smaller needles (#6) and work k1, p1 rib for 2 inches. Bind off all sts loosely in pattern.

FINISHING

Sew the side seams tog on the wrong side.

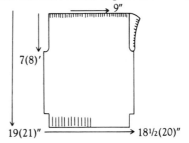

9"

7(8)'

19(21)"   18½(20)"

16

Burning Bush

SIZES: Small, medium; medium size is in
  parentheses

FINISHED MEASUREMENTS: Bust 42
  (46) inches; total length 27 inches

MATERIALS:
  Stacy Charles Buffo 11 (12) (50 g/1.75
    ounce) skeins, red
  Needles: #11 single-point, #10½ 24-inch
    circular

GAUGE: 10 sts and 14 rows = 4 inches
      (2.5 sts = 1 inch; 3.5 rows = 1
      inch)

STITCH PATTERNS:
  #1: Stockinette stitch
  #2: Braided cable worked over 12 sts as
    follows:

  Row 1: k12.
  Row 2: p12.
  Row 3: *place 3 sts on cable needle and hold
    in front of work, k the next 3 sts, k3 from
    c n*. Repeat 1× more.
  Rows 4, 5, 6, 7, 8: k the k sts and p the p sts.
  Row 9: k3, place 3 sts on c n and hold in back
    of work, k next 3 sts, k3 from c n, k3.
  Rows 10, 11, 12: k the k sts and p the p sts.
  Row 13: Repeat from row 3.

NOTE: When knitting, try to pull all slubs
  and long hair to the right (knit) side of
  the work.

BACK

With #11 needles, cast on 54 (60) sts. Work in
st st until work measures 15 inches; place coil or
yarn markers at each edge. Continue in pattern
until work measures 25 inches. Bind off all sts
loosely.

FRONT

Work same as for back, placing markers when
piece measures 15 inches. Work until piece measures 22 inches. Shape the neck: Work 18 (21)
sts. Attach a new skein of yarn and loosely bind
off the center 18 sts; work across the last 18 (21)
sts. Working each side with a separate skein of
yarn, dec 1 st at each neck edge 2× (16 [19] sts).
Continue to work until the piece measures the
same as the back. Bind off all sts loosely.

SLEEVES

With #11 needles, cast on 32 sts. Working in st
st, inc 1 st each edge on every 6th row until 54
(58) sts. Work until sleeve measures 17 (18)
inches. Bind off all sts very loosely.

BOTTOM BAND

Cast on 12 sts and work the cable pattern for 40
inches. Bind off all sts loosely in pattern.

FINISHING

1. Sew shoulder seams tog.
2. With #10½ circular needle, pick up 60 sts around neck and, knitting only, work until cowl measures 10 inches. Bind off all sts loosely.

3. Attach sleeves to body of sweater, placing them in space between markers. Sew.
4. Sew side seams and sleeve seams.
5. Sew sides of bottom band tog. Attach the cable to the bottom of the sweater, easing the body of the sweater to fit the length of the cable braid. Sew.

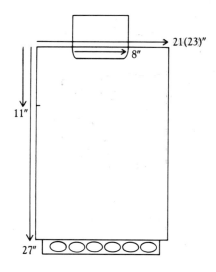

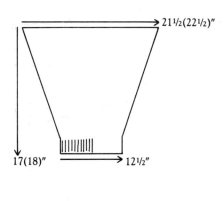

Classic Cable Vest

SIZES: Medium, large; large size is in parentheses

FINISHED MEASUREMENTS: Chest 46 (48) inches; total length 24 (26) inches

MATERIALS:

Lane Borgosesia Volley 5 (6) (50 g/1.75 ounce) skeins, brown

Needles: #4, #6 single-point; #4 31-inch circular

Stitch holders

GAUGE: 20 sts and 28 rows = 4 inches
(5 sts = 1 inch; 7 rows = 1 inch)

STITCH PATTERNS:

#1: Stockinette stitch

#2: Fancy cable pattern worked over 12 sts as follows:

Rows 1, 5: p2, k8, p2.

Row 2 and all even-numbered rows: k2, p8, k2.

Row 3: p2, sl 2 sts onto a c n and hold at the front of work, k2, then k2 from the c n, slip 2 sts on c n and hold at the back of the work, k2, then k2 from the c n, p2.

Row 7: p2, slip 2 sts onto c n and hold at back of work, k2, then k2 from the c n, sl 2 sts onto c n and hold at front of work, k2, then k2 from c n, p2.

Row 9: Repeat from row 1.

BACK

With smaller needles (#4), cast on 116 (126) sts. Work in k2, p2 rib for 2½ inches. Change to larger needles (#6) and pattern stitch #1. Work in pattern for 11½ inches (14 inches including rib). At the beg of the next 2 rows bind off 8 sts (100 [110] sts). Work straight until the armholes measure 9 inches. Now shape the shoulders as follows: Bind off 15 sts at the beg of the next 4 rows. On the large size, bind off 5 sts at the beg of the next 2 rows. Place the remaining 40 sts on a st holder.

LEFT FRONT

With smaller needles (#4), cast on 56 (62) sts. Work in k2, p2 rib for 2½ inches. Change to larger needles (#6) and pattern stitch #1. Work for 3½ inches in pattern (6 inches including rib).

Work pockets as follows: For the pocket linings (make 2), with larger needles (#6), cast on 22 sts. Work 5 inches in pattern stitch #1. Set aside the 2 pieces. On the vest front work k16 (18) sts, *p2, k2*, p2 across the next 22 sts, turn, working across the center 22 sts only until this border measures 1½ inches. Bind off all 22 sts loosely in pattern. Reattach the yarn to the remaining sts to the left of this border and k18 (22) sts. Turn, p18 (22) sts, place the 22 sts of the pocket lining into the space, the purl rows facing you, and purl these 22 sts, p16 (18) sts.

Work in pattern stitch #1 until the front measures 12 inches total. At the neck edge, begin pattern stitch #2 across the first 12 sts. Working in pattern stitches #1 and #2 simultaneously, work until the front measures 14 inches. Bind off 8 sts at the armhole edge. Begin to shape the neck edge as follows: Maintain the first 12 sts in pattern, dec 1 st, and work to the end of the row. Dec 1 st every 4th row (work 3 rows and then the dec row) in this manner 15× more. Work until the armhole measures 9 inches and shape the shoulders as follows: From the armhole edge only, bind off 16 (16) sts 2×. On the large size, bind off an additional 6 sts 1×.

RIGHT FRONT

Repeat this front piece, reversing all the shapings.

FINISHING

1. With the right sides of back and fronts facing, sew the shoulder seams, straightening out the slanted edge.
2. With the #4 31-inch circular needle and the right side facing you, pick up all the sts around the neck and work in k2, p2 rib for 4 rows. Now space 6 buttonholes 2 inches apart, starting the first buttonhole 2 sts from the bottom left-side edge. Continue to work in k2, p2 rib for 4 more rows. Bind off all sts loosely in pattern.
3. With the wrong sides facing you, sew the pocket lining and the pocket rib.
4. With smaller needles, and the right side facing you, pick up 112 sts around the armhole. Work k2, p2 rib for 10 rows. Bind off all the stitches loosely in pattern.
5. With the right sides facing, sew the side seams.

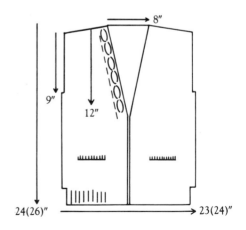

22

23

Jay's Grid

SIZES: Small, medium; medium size is in
  parentheses
FINISHED MEASUREMENTS: Chest
  42 (45) inches; total length 25 (26) inches
MATERIALS:
  Using one strand of each A and B held
    together
  (A) Stacy Charles Vespucci 8 (9) (50
    g/1.75 ounce) skeins, navy
  (b) Melrose Pietra 7 (8) (50 g/1.75 ounce)
    skeins, gray-blue
  Needles #7, #9 single-point; #7 16-inch
    circular
  Stitch holders
GAUGE: 16 sts and 22 rows = 4 inches
           (4 sts = 1 inch; 5.5 rows = 1
           inch)
Make your swatch using larger needles and
stitch pattern #1 (basket stitch).
STITCH PATTERNS:
  #1: Basket Stitch
  Rows 1, 7: Knit.
  Rows 2, 8: Purl.
  Rows 3, 5: *k1, p4, k1*. Repeat * to *.
  Rows 4, 6: *p1, k4, p1*. Repeat * to *.
  Rows 9, 11: *p2, k2, p2*. Repeat * to *.
  Rows 10, 12: *k2, p2, k2*. Repeat
    * to *.
  Repeat rows 1–12 for the pattern.

  #2: 2×4 Rib
  Row 1: *k2, p4*. Repeat * to *.
  Row 2: *p2, k4*. Repeat * to *.
  Repeat rows 1 and 2 for pattern.

BACK

With smaller needles (#7), cast on 84 (90) sts.
Work k2, p2 rib for 3 inches. Change to larger
needles (#9) and pattern stitch #1, and work
until the back measures 15 inches. Place yarn
markers at each edge. Continue in pattern until
the back measures 24½ (25½) inches. Shape the
shoulders as follows: Bind off loosely 13 sts at the
beg of the next 4 rows. Place the remaining 32 sts
on a st holder.

FRONT

Work the same as for the back until the front
measures 22 (23) inches in total. Shape the neck
as follows: Work 32 (35) sts; place the center 20
sts on a st holder. Attach another skein of yarn
(A and B held together) and, working each side
separately, dec 1 st at each neck edge every knit
row 6× (26 [29] sts). Work until front measures
24½ (25½) inches, and shape the shoulders by
binding off 13 sts at the beg of the next 2 outer-
edge rows and 13 (16) sts at the beg of the next 2
outer-edge rows.

SLEEVES

With smaller needles (#7), cast on 26 (30) sts. Work k2, p2 rib for 3 inches. On the last rib row, inc 10 sts evenly across (36 [40] sts). Working in pattern stitch #2, change to larger needles (#9) and inc 1 st at each edge on every 4th row (work 3 rows and then the inc row) 22 × (80 [84] sts). Work until the sleeve measures 21 (22) inches in total. Bind off all sts loosely.

FINISHING

1. With right sides of back and front facing each other, sew the shoulder seams.

2. With right sides facing, place the sleeve into the space between the markers and sew.
3. Fold the sweater so that the wrong side is facing out; sew the side seams and the sleeve seams.
4. With #7 16-inch circular needle, starting at the left shoulder seam, with the right side facing you, pick up 14 sts at the left front edge, k the 20 sts from the st holder, pick up 14 sts on the right front edge, k the 32 sts from the st holder. Work in k2, p2 rib until the neck rib measures 1 inch. Bind off loosely in pattern, attaching the last st to the first bound-off st.

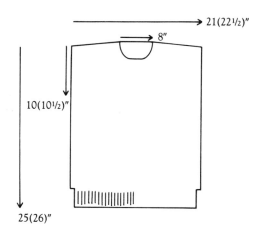

21(22½)"

8"

10(10½)"

25(26)"

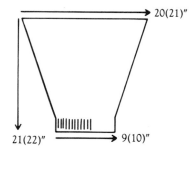

20(21)"

21(22)"

9(10)"

INTERMEDIATE

Joy

SIZES: Small, medium; medium size is in parentheses

FINISHED MEASUREMENTS: Bust 40 (42) inches; total length 26 inches

MATERIALS:

Lane Borgosesia Dream 10 (50 g/1.75 ounce) skeins, green

For sleeves, use 4 more skeins

Needles: #7, #8 single-point; #7 31-inch circular

Stitch holder

GAUGE: 16 sts and 20 rows = 4 inches
        (4 sts = 1 inch; 5 rows = 1 inch)

STITCH PATTERNS:

#1: Seed Stitch

Row 1: k1, p1.

Row 2: p1, k1.

Repeat rows 1 and 2.

#2: Cable pattern

Rows 1, 3, 5, 7, 9 (w s): p4, k4, p12, k4, p4, k4, p4, seed st 16 (20) sts, p4, k4, p4, k4, p12, k4, p4.

Row 2 (r s): k4, p4, *slip 3 sts to c n and hold in the back, k3, then k3 from the c n, slip next 3 sts to c n and hold in front, k3, then k3 from the c n,* p4, k4, p4, k4, seed st 16 (20) sts, k4, p4, k4, p4, repeat from * to *, p4, k4.

Rows 4, 6, 8, 10: knit the knits, purl the purls, seed the seed sts. Repeat rows 1–10 for the pattern.

BACK

With smaller needles (#7), cast on 88 (92) sts. Work k1, p1 rib for 2 inches, finishing with a r s row. With w s facing, use larger (#8) needles to set up patterns 1 and 2 as in row 1 of pattern stitch #2. Continue to work in pattern until piece measures 10 inches in total. Now inc 1 st at each edge of work every 4th row (work 3 rows then the increase row) 8×, working these increases in seed st. Continue across 104 (108) sts until the armhole measures 16 inches. Shape the shoulders by loosely binding off 10 sts at the beg of the next 6 rows (44 [48] sts remain). Bind off 7 (9) sts at the beg of the next 2 rows. Place the remaining 30 sts on a st holder.

FRONT

Work same as for the back until the armhole measures 4 inches (92 [96] sts). Work 34 (36) sts, attach a new skein of yarn, bind off the center 24 sts, and work the last 34 (36) sts. Working each side with a separate skein of yarn, dec 1 st at each neck edge every 3rd row (work 2 rows then the increase row) 3×. AT THE SAME TIME continue to increase at the armhole edge. Work until the

armhole measures 16 inches. Shape the shoulders the same as the back shaping.

Sew the shoulder seams tog.

COLLAR

With #7 31-inch circular needle, pick up around the neck 176 sts. Work in seed stitch for 8 inches. Bind off all sts loosely in pattern.

If you want to change the vest into a pullover, here are the instructions.

SLEEVES

With smaller needles (#7), cast on 40 sts. Work in k1, p1 rib for 2 inches. Change to larger needles (#8) and pattern stitch #1. Inc 1 st at each edge of every 5th row (work 4 rows and then the dec row) 16×. Work across 72 sts until the sleeve measures 18 inches in total. Bind off all sts loosely in pattern.

FINISHING

1. With right sides facing, attach sleeve to sweater, measuring a 9-inch armhole. Sew.
2. With wrong side facing you, sew the side seams and the sleeve seams.

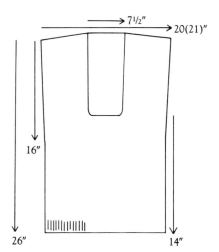

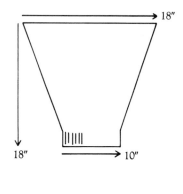

Check-It-Up

SIZES: Small, medium; medium size is in parentheses

FINISHED MEASUREMENTS: Bust 43 (47) inches; total length 22½ (24½) inches

MATERIALS:
- (A) Aarlan Flou 4 (50 g/1.75 ounce) skeins, Kelly green
- (B) Aarlan Flou 4 (50 g/1.75 ounce) skeins, gray
- (C) Pingouin Contrastes 1 (50 g/1.75 ounce) skein, yellow
- (D) Pingouin Contrastes 1 (50 g/1.75/ ounce) skein, fuschia
- (E) Berger du Nord Pele-Mele 1 (50 g/1.75 ounce) skein, green/pink

Needles: #9, #10 single-point

Crochet hook F

Large embroidery needle for duplicate stitch

Stitch holders

Buttons and shoulder pads

GAUGE: 12 sts and 16 rows = 4 inches (3 sts = 1 inch; 4 rows = 1 inch)

STITCH PATTERN:
With A, work 4 rows st st.
With B, work 4 rows st st.

BACK

With #10 needles and A, cast on 64 (70) sts. Work k2, p2 rib for 4 rows. Change to B and st st and work in pattern stitch until piece measures 11 (12) inches in total. At the beg of the next two rows, bind off 2 (3) sts (60 [64] sts). Continuing in pattern, dec 1 st at each edge every 3rd row (work 2 rows and then the dec row) 16 (18) ×. The armhole should measure 11½ inches and 28 sts remain. Place these sts on a st holder.

RIGHT FRONT

With #10 needles and A, cast on 34 (38) sts. Work k2, p2 rib for 4 rows. Change to B and st st. Work in pattern stitch until piece measures 11 (12) inches. At the armhole edge, bind off 2 (3) sts. While working in pattern, dec 1 st at the armhole edge every 3rd row (work 2 rows and then the dec row) 16 (18) ×. When the armhole measures 9½ (10½) inches, shape the neck as follows: At the neck edge, bind off 10 sts. Then, at the neck edge, dec 1 st on every row 6×. *Remember to continue armhole decreasing as before.* Armhole should measure 11½ inches and 0 sts remain.

LEFT FRONT

Make second front piece, reversing the shaping.

SLEEVES

With #10 needles and A, cast on 30 sts. Work

k2, p2 rib for 4 rows. Change to B and st st and, working in pattern, inc 1 st at each edge on every 4th row (work 3 rows and then the inc row) 14 (17) × (56 [62] sts). Work until sleeve measures 15 (16) inches. Shape raglan sleeve cap as follows: At the beg of the next 2 rows, bind off 2 (3) sts. Working in pattern, dec 1 st at each edge on every 3rd row (work 2 rows and then the dec row) 14 (16) × until 24 sts remain and the armhole measures 11½ (12½) inches. Place these sts on a st holder.

Make 2 sleeves.

DUPLICATE STITCH

Work the duplicate stitch before sewing the pieces tog. With double strand of D and embroidery needle, at the 13th st from the right edge of each sleeve, work 1 row of vertical duplicate st. With E and size F crochet hook, work 1 vertical row of sl st on the 15th st from the edge. With double strand of A and embroidery needle, on the 13th st from the left edge, work 1 row of vertical duplicate st. *There should be 1 vertical stitch in between each of these 3 rows of work.* Using double strand of A, on the front, 8 sts from the side edge, work 1 row of vertical duplicate st. On the 10th st from the side edge, with E and size F crochet hook, work 1 row vertical sl st. With double strand of D, on the 12th st from the side edge, work 1 row vertical duplicate st. Repeat these 3 rows, starting 4 sts from the front edge, in the same sequence. Repeat these 6 stripes on the opposite front piece, remembering to reverse the colors.

Work horizontal duplicate st on all pieces of the garment above every second green stripe (on the gray row) with a double strand of C.

FINISHING

When you have completed all the duplicate st, sew the armhole seams and the side seams and the sleeve seams. *Do not remove the st holders yet.* When all the seams have been sewn, place all remaining sts on the #9 needles.

NECKBAND

With #9 needles and A, pick up 13 sts along the right front edge. Across the next 24 sts of the sleeve, k3 tog 8 × (8 sts). Across the 28 sts of the back, k2 tog 14 × (14 sts). Across the next 24 sts of the sleeve, k3 tog 8 × (8 sts). Pick up 13 sts along left front edge (56 sts). Work in k2, p2 rib for 4 inches. Bind off all sts loosely and fold band inward, sewing the bound-off edge to the seam formed by picking up the sts. *Sew loosely.*

FRONT BANDS

With #9 needles and A, pick up 80 sts along the left front edge. Work k2, p2 rib for 6 rows. Bind off all sts loosely in pattern.

On the right front band, on the 3rd row of the k2, p2 rib, space 9 buttonholes 14 sts apart.

Begin the first buttonhole 2 sts from the edge. Work this band the same length as the other band, binding off all sts loosely in pattern.

Sew on the buttons. Center the shoulder pads and sew.

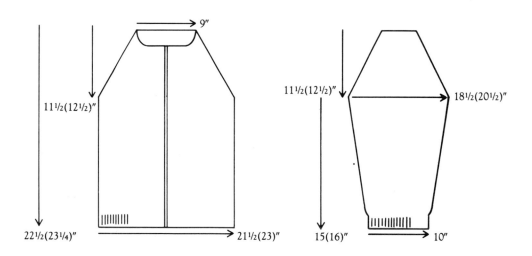

Positive/Negative

SIZES: One size

FINISHED MEASUREMENTS: Bust 44 inches; total length 21 inches

MATERIALS:

- (A) Stacy Charles Valentino #306 3 (100 g/3.5 ounce) skeins, natural
- (B) Berger du Nord Coton #5 2 (50 g/1.75 ounce) skeins, black
- (C) Knitting Fever Noro Katoreya 1 (50 g/1.75 ounce) skein, natural

Needles: #8, #9 single-point; #8 24-inch circular

GAUGE: 16 sts and 20 rows = 4 inches
(4 sts = 1 inch; 5 rows = 1 inch)

STITCH PATTERNS:

- #1: Stockinette stitch
- #2: Reverse stockinette stitch

BACK

With #8 needles and B, cast on 88 sts. Starting with a purl row, work 3 rows rev st st. Change to #9 needles and A and, starting with 1 row purl, work in st st for 3 inches. With A, k46; with B, p42. Turn your work, k42 in B and p46 in A. *Remember to twist yarns when changing color.* Turn work, k46 in A, p4 in B, and with C p38. Turn, k38 in C, k4 in B, and p46 in A. Turn, k46 in A, p42 in B. Turn, k42 in B and p46 in A. With A, work in st st for 3½ inches. With B, p51; with A,

k37. Turn, p37 and k51. Repeat these 2 rows 1 more time. Work with A in st st for 2 inches. When the work measures 11 inches, place markers at each edge to indicate armhole. With B, p34; with A, k54. Turn, work sts as they face you. Turn; with C, p30; with B, p4; with A, k54. Turn, work sts as they face you. Turn; with B, p34; with A, k54. Turn, work sts as they face you. With A, work in st st until piece measures 19 inches. Shape the neck as follows: With A, work 31 sts. Attach a new skein of yarn and bind off the center 26 sts, work last 31 sts. Working each side separately, at the neck edge, dec 1 st each row 3×. Work until the piece measures 21 inches or the desired length. Bind off all sts loosely.

FRONT

Work the same as the back until the piece measures 16 inches. Work neck shaping as the back neck. Work until the front measures the same as the back. Bind off all sts loosely.

SLEEVES

Sew shoulder seams tog. With #9 needles and A, pick up 72 sts in the space between markers. Dec 1 st each side on every knit row until 66 sts remain and the sleeve measures 1½ inches.

Change to #8 needles and B, and work 3 rows in rev st st. Bind off all sts loosely.

NECKBAND

With #8 24-inch circular needle and B, pick up 98 sts around the neck. Work 3 rounds in purl only. Bind off all sts loosely.

FINISHING

With the right sides facing each other, sew side seams and sleeve seams.

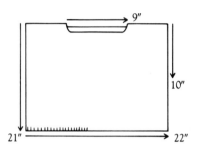

True Blue

SIZES: Medium, large; large size is in parentheses

FINISHED MEASUREMENTS: Chest 45 (48) inches; total length 25 (26) inches

MATERIALS:

Knitting Fever Superworsted 12 (14) (50 g/1.75 ounce) skeins, blue

Needles: #4, #7 single-point; #4 16-inch circular

Stitch holders

GAUGE: 18 sts and 28 rows = 4 inches
    (4.5 sts = 1 inch; 7 rows = 1 inch)

Make 2 swatches using larger needles and both stitch patterns.

STITCH PATTERNS:

#1: Woven Stitch

Row 1: k1 *k2, yf, sl1, yb*. Repeat from * to *. End k2, k1.

Row 2: purl.

Repeat rows 1 and 2 for the pattern.

When slipping, do not pull the thread too tightly.

#2: Corncob Cable Stitch

Row 1: p2, k9, p2.

Row 2 and all even-numbered rows: k2, p9, k2.

Row 3: p2, place 1 st on c n and hold in front of the work, k3, k1 from the c n, k1, place 3 sts on c n and hold at the back of the work, k1, k3 from c n, p2.

Repeat rows 1–3 for the pattern.

BACK

With smaller needles (#4), cast on 94 (100) sts. Work k1, p1 rib for 3 inches. On the last rib row, inc 9 sts evenly spaced across the row (103 [109] sts). Change to larger needles (#7) and pattern stitch #1 and work until the piece measures 14 (15) inches in total. Place yarn markers at each edge. Continue in pattern until the back measures 25 (26) inches in total. Bind off all sts loosely.

FRONT

Work the front the same as the back until the piece measures 23 (24) inches in total. Shape the neck as follows: Work 41 (44) sts, place the center 21 sts on a st holder, attach a new skein of yarn, and work the last 41 (44) sts. Working both sides separately, at each neck edge dec 1 st on every r s row 6× (35 [38] sts remain). Continue until the front measures the same as the back. Bind off all sts loosely in pattern.

SLEEVES

With smaller needles (#4), cast on 56 sts. Work

k1, p1 rib for 3 inches. On the last rib row, inc 11 sts evenly across the row (67 sts). Change to larger needles (#7) and pattern stitches #1 and #2, setting them up as follows:

1. Remember to bring the yb and yf after every sl st.

2. Maintain 1 k st at each edge on every row.

Row 1: k2, sl 1, k2, p2, k9, p2, k2, sl 1, k2, sl 1, k2, p2, k9, p2, k2, sl 1, k2, sl 1, k2, p2, k9, p2, k2, sl 1, k2. Start and end the row with an edge (knit) st (67 sts).

Row 2: Work the sts as specified on row 2 of each pattern stitch. Maintaining the combination of the pattern stitches, inc 1 st at each edge on every 5th row (work 4 rows and then the inc row) 20× (105 sts). Work until the sleeve measures 21 (22) inches. Bind off 45 sts loosely. Work across the next 15 sts in pattern. Bind off the last 45 sts loosely. Reattach the yarn to the remaining 15 sts and, working in pattern, continue on this cable strip until it measures 8 inches. Bind off all sts loosely.

FINISHING

1. With right sides of back and front facing, sew the shoulder seams.

2. With right sides facing, place the sleeves into the space between the markers, leaving the cable strip hanging on the inside of the garment.

3. Fold the sweater and sew the side seams and the sleeve seams.

4. Easing the cable strip, attach it to the neck edge, covering the shoulder seam. Sew the strip flat on both sides.

5. With #4 16-inch circular needle, starting at the beg of the left cable strip, pick up 4 sts across the cable, pick up 18 sts across the left front edge, knit 21 sts from the st holder, pick up 18 sts across the right front edge, pick up 4 sts across the right cable, pick up 42 sts across the back neck edge. In k1, p1 rib, work until the neck rib measures 2½ inches. Bind off all the sts loosely in pattern, joining the first and last bound-off st to form a smooth edge.

6. Fold the neck rib toward the inside of the sweater and sew it down loosely. Make sure it is loose enough for a head to pass through.

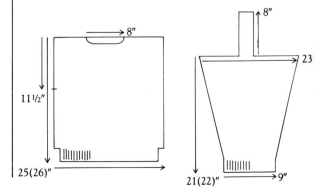

ADVANCED

Jolie Blanche

SIZES: Medium, large; large size is in
parentheses
FINISHED MEASUREMENTS: Bust 37
(44) inches; total length 23 (25) inches
MATERIALS:
China silk Imari 5 (100 g/3.5 ounce)
skeins, natural
Needles: #7, #8 single-point, #7 24-inch
circular
GAUGE: 18 sts and 24 rows = 4 inches
(4.5 sts = 1 inch; 6 rows = 1
inch)
STITCH PATTERN:
#1. Stockinette stitch
#2. Cable and Ladder Pattern
Multiple of 14 sts + 1
Row 1 (w s) and all other w s rows: k1,
p2 tog, yo, p11, k1. Repeat from
* to *.
Row 2: k1, *ssk, yo, sl next 3 sts to c n
and hold in back, k3, k3 from c n, k6*.
Repeat from * to *.
Row 4: k1, *ssk, yo, k12*. Repeat from *
to *.
Row 6: k1, *ssk, yo, k3, sl next 3 sts to c
n and hold in front, k3, then k3 from c
n, k3*. Repeat.
Row 8: Repeat row 4.
Repeat rows 1–8.

BACK

With smaller needles (#7), cast on 85 (99) sts.
Work pattern stitch #2 for 48 rows plus row 1 (6
repeats of the pattern plus 1 row). Change to
larger needles (#8) and st st and work until
sweater measures 13 (15) inches. At the beg of
the next 2 rows, bind off 20 sts (45 [59] sts).
Work straight until armhole measures 10 inches.
Bind off all sts loosely.

FRONT

With smaller needles (#7), cast on 43 (57) sts.
Work 48 rows plus row 1. Change to st st and
larger needles (#8). Work 2 (4) inches, and start
shaping for V neck. At the neck edge, dec 1 st
on the next row and every following 6th row
(work 5 rows and then the dec row) 13×. Work
until piece measures 13 (15) inches and bind off
20 sts at the armhole edge. *At the same time,*
remember to continue the neck shaping. When
10 sts remain and the front measures the same as
the back, bind off all sts loosely.

FINISHING

With right sides of back and front together, sew
shoulder seams.

ARMHOLE CABLES

Do not sew side seams. With smaller needles (#7) and right sides facing, pick up 85 (99) sts along front and back armhole from the corners. Now work pattern stitch #2 for 4 inches. Bind off all sts loosely.

Sew side seams together.

Sew cable edge to bottom armhole edge.

NECKBAND

With #7 24-inch circular needle, pick up 183 (197) sts around the entire neck. Work pattern stitch #2 for 3 inches. Bind off all sts loosely.

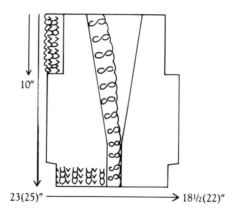

10"

23(25)" ⟶ 18½(22)"

White Dalmatian

SIZES: Small, medium; medium size is in parentheses

FINISHED MEASUREMENTS: Bust 40 (44) inches; total length 23½ (25) inches

MATERIALS:

(A) W. West Designs Aspen 10 (50 g/1.75 ounce) skeins, écru

(B) Stacy Charles Buffo 1 (50 g/1.75 ounce) skein, écru

Needles: #10, #11 single-point; #10 16-inch circular

Stitch holder

GAUGE: 12 sts and 16 rows = 4 inches (3 sts = 1 inch; 4 rows = 1 inch)

STITCH PATTERN: Stockinette stitch

SPECIAL INSTRUCTIONS: This sweater is knitted in one piece.

When working with B, pull all long hair and slubs to the right side of the work.

SLEEVE

With #11 needles and A, cast on 40 (46) sts. Working in st st, inc 1 st at each edge every 6th row (work 5 rows and then the inc row) until 54 (60) sts. Place markers here. When sleeve measures 6 inches, using B, start the first spot #1, following the graph, 16 sts from the beginning of the row. Work with 3 skeins of yarn, twisting threads to connect them and to prevent holes.

When work measures 12 (13) inches, inc 1 st at each edge on every knit row 16 (16) × (86 [92] sts). Piece measures 18 (19) inches.

BACK AND FRONT

At the beginning of the next 2 rows, cast on 22 sts (130 [136] sts). At each edge on every knit row, inc 1 st 6× (142 [148] sts). Continue to work straight until piece, from 22 st cast-on edge, measures 5½ (6½) inches. Now divide work for the neck: Work across 71 (74) sts, placing the remaining sts on a st holder. Work this piece for 9 inches. Now work the 71 (74) sts from the st holder until this piece also measures 9 inches. Working across all stitches, work 10 rows and then, using B, work spot #2, following the graph. When piece measures 3 (4) inches from completed neck, dec 1 st at each edge of every knit row 6× (130 [136] sts). Bind off 22 sts at the beg of the next 2 rows (86 [92] sts). Using B, begin spot #3 34 sts from the right edge 8 rows after the completed spot #2.

SLEEVE

Dec 1 st at each edge on every knit row until 54 (60) sts remain. Work straight until this sleeve measures same as first sleeve at marker. Dec 1 st at each edge on every 6th row (work 5 rows and then the dec row) until 40 (46) sts remain and sleeves measure the same length. Bind off all sts loosely.

FINISHING

With #10 needles and A, pick up 96 sts along the front bottom edge. Work 4 rows rev st st (first row is a knit row). Bind off loosely. Repeat for the other side.

NECKBAND

With #10 circular needle and A, pick up 76 sts around the neck. Work 4 rounds of purl. Bind off all sts loosely.

With the right sides facing, sew the side seams and the sleeve seams.

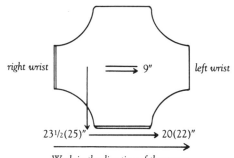

right wrist   9"   *left wrist*

23½(25)"   20(22)"

*Each square represents
5 stitches and 5 rows.*

Work in the direction of the arrow.

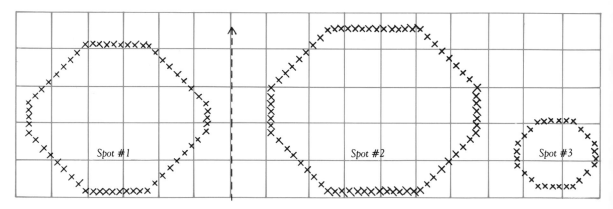

Spot #1   Spot #2   Spot #3

46

Black Rainbow

SIZES: Small, medium; medium size is in parentheses

FINISHED MEASUREMENTS: Bust 38 (40) inches; total length 20 (21) inches

MATERIALS:

(A) Anny Blatt Angor'anny 28 (30) 20 g/.7 ounce) skeins, black

(B) Rainbow Mills Butterfly Silk 1 (50 g/1.75 ounce) skein multicolor

Needles: #7 single-point; #7 24-inch circular; #9 31-inch circular

Stitch holder

GAUGE: 16 sts and 20 rows = 4 inches
(4 sts = 1 inch; 5 rows = 1 inch)

STITCH PATTERN:

Stockinette stitch

SPECIAL INSTRUCTIONS:

Use Butterfly Silk in st st whenever you want to. I cut approximately 12-inch-long pieces and worked it in 1 row of knit for about 7 inches and on the following purl row for the remaining length.

The sweater is made in 1 piece.

SLEEVE

With #7 single-point needles and double strand of A, cast on 34 sts. Work k1, p1 rib for 3 inches. Change to #9 needles, and on the first k row inc 6 sts evenly across the row (40 sts). Working in st st, inc 1 st each edge every 4th row (work 3 rows and then the inc row) until 64 sts. Place marker at last increase. Work straight until the piece measures 12 (13) inches. Place marker. Inc 1 st at each edge every knit row until 116 sts.

BACK AND FRONT

At the beginning of the next 2 rows, cast on 24 (28) sts (164 [172] sts). Work straight for 5 (6) inches. Divide the work for the neck: Work across 82 (86) sts. Place remaining sts on a st holder. Work for 9 inches. Place these sts on a st holder and work across the sts that were formerly on a holder until this piece measures 9 inches as well. This division forms the neck opening. Now join the 2 pieces by knitting all the sts. Work for 5 (6) inches. At the beginning of the next 2 rows, bind off 24 (28) sts.

SECOND SLEEVE

At each edge, dec 1 st on every k row until 64 sts. Place marker at last decrease. Work straight for the same length as opposite sleeve, measured between markers. Place marker. Dec 1 st at each edge on every 4th row (work 3 rows and then the dec row) until 40 sts remain and this sleeve measures the same as the first sleeve. On the last purl row, dec 6 sts evenly across the row. Change

49

to #7 single-point needles and k1, p1 rib, and work for 3 inches. Bind off all sts loosely in pattern.

FINISHING

Sew sleeve seams and side seams.

With #7 circular needle, pick up 80 sts on the front and 80 sts on the back bottom edges. Work in k1, p1 rib across 160 sts for 3 inches. Bind off all sts loosely in pattern.

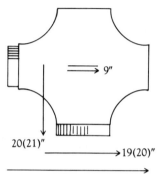

20(21)″

9″

19(20)″

Work in the direction of the arrow.

Swing High

SIZES: One size

FINISHED MEASUREMENTS: Bust 46 inches; total length 25 inches

MATERIALS:

  (A) Knitting Fever/Noro Yamato 14 (16) (50 g/1.75 ounce) skeins, brown/rust

  (B) Crystal Palace Loop de Loop 4 (50 g/1.75 ounce) skeins, multi

  Needles: #8, #10 single-point; #8 16-inch circular

  Bobbins

GAUGE: 14 sts and 16 rows = 4 inches (3.5 sts = 1 inch; 4 rows = 1 inch)

STITCH PATTERN:

  Stockinette stitch

BACK

With smaller needles (#8) and A, cast on 58 sts. Work k1, p1 rib for 3 inches. Change to larger needles (#10) and st st, and inc 10 sts evenly across the first k row (68 sts). Purl 1 row. Now begin incorporating B, wrapped on bobbins, as follows:

Row 1: With A, k8; with B, k2, with A, k21 (pulling A tightly behind B to create a ridge), with B, k2; with A, k2; with B, k2; with A, k21; with B, k2; with A, k8.

Row 2: With A and B in pattern as established, p all sts.

Row 3: With A, k1, inc 1, k6; with B, k2; with A, k21; with B, k2; with A, k4; with B, k2; with A, k21; with B, k2; with A, k6, inc 1, k1.

Row 4: In pattern, purl all sts.

Row 5: Knit in pattern.

Row 6: Repeat row 4.

Row 7: Inc 1 st at each edge, also moving B 1 st to the right on the first 2 stripes and 1 st to the left on the second group of color stripes.

Repeat rows 2–7, moving B on every 7th row. Work in this manner until 84 sts and piece measures 13 inches.

Now add 2 new B bobbins as follows:

Knit row: With A, k8; with B, k2; with A, k9; with B, k3; with A, k9; with B, k2; with A, k18; with B, k2; with A, k9; with B, k3; with A, k9; with B, k2; with A, k8.

Purl row: In pattern, work all sts.

Knit row: Work in pattern, moving new bobbins 1 st to the right, adding a new A bobbin, 1 st to the left. Continue in this manner until the center section between the new bobbins, contains 7 A sts.

Note: When the sweater measures 15 inches, place yarn markers at each edge.
Maintaining the pattern, no longer moving the bobbins, work until the piece measures 25 inches in total. Loosely bind off all sts, using A.

FRONT

Work as for the back, until the piece measures 23 inches. Divide for the neck. Work the first 28 sts in pattern, attach a new skein of A, bind off the center 28 sts, and work the last 28 sts in pattern. On the following k row, dec 1 st at the neck edge. Work until the front measures the same as the back. Bind off all sts loosely.

SLEEVES

With smaller needles (#8) and A, cast on 36 sts. Work in k1, p1 rib for 3 inches. Change to larger needles (#10) and st st, increasing 12 sts evenly across the first k row (48 sts). Working in pattern, inc 1 st at each edge on every 4th row (work 3 rows and then the inc row) 16× until 80 sts. Work until the sleeve measures 17–18 inches. Bind off all sts loosely.

FINISHING

1. With the right sides of back and front facing, sew the shoulder seams.
2. With the right sides facing, place the sleeves in the space between the markers and sew.
3. Fold the sweater and, with the wrong side facing you, sew the side seams and the sleeve seams.
4. With the right side facing you, with #8 16-inch circular needle, starting at the left shoulder seam, pick up 10 sts, pick up center front 28 sts, pick up 10 sts on the right shoulder edge, pick up center back 28 sts. Work in k1, p1 rib for 4 inches or desired length. Bind off all sts loosely in pattern, attaching the first and last sts to avoid a hole.

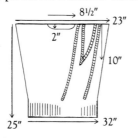

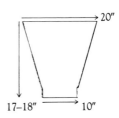

52

NOTE:

All yarns used in this book can be ordered from

Gwen Byrne
529 Amsterdam Avenue
New York, N.Y. 10024

All sweaters are also available custom-made. Request a price list, enclosing a stamped, self-addressed envelope.